ιmre
Service

Identifying your World War I Soldier from Badges and Photographs

IAIN SWINNERTON

With illustrations by

ROLAND SYMONS

Published by the
Federation of Family History Societies (Publications) Ltd
Units 15-16 Chesham Industrial Estate
Oram Street, Bury, Lancashire BL9 6EN

First edition 2001
Reprinted with amendments 2006

Copyright © Iain Swinnerton

CIRCULATIO
DRL   11/0

ISBN 1 86006 128 1

Printed and bound by The Alden Group, Oxford and Northampton.

CONTENTS

A typical photograph of a smart young pre-war soldier (it was actually taken in 1912) in his walking-out dress. The cap and collar badges clearly identify him as belonging to the 16th Lancers.

INTRODUCTION

Events that have taken place since 1996 have resulted in an unprecedented rise in interest in tracing the careers of soldiers who fought in World War I. These include the 80th anniversary of the Battle of the Somme in 1996, together with the release of officers' personal documents in the same year; the 80th anniversary of the end of the Great War in 1998 and the ongoing release of soldiers' documents since then.

The most important thing to know when conducting such a search is the regiment or corps in which the soldier served, but so often, this is not known. However, over the years, many people have shown me pictures of their ancestors and asked me to identify the unit and I have found the photograph contained features which would have allowed them to do so themselves, had they had access to the right sources.

These can be anything from the ubiquitous cap badge to collar badges, arm, rank, service and proficiency badges or particular items of individual regimental dress. Photographs are often faded and indistinct, but often the mere outline shape of a cap or collar badge will suffice to identify the regiment.

Although there have been many good books published on most of these subjects, many are now out of print and those that remain, which are listed in the bibliography at the end of this book, are often expensive and may not be easy to obtain. The aim of this book, intended to be a companion to the three books on tracing World War One Ancestry by Norman Holding, also published by the Federation of Family History Societies, is to draw together in one volume as many as possible of the various badges and devices used during that conflict, and so help the reader to ascertain the unit in which the ancestor served.

All the photographs in the book have been loaned from the Jervis WWI Photographic Index for which my grateful thanks go to Mr Simon Jervis.

All the additional illustrations to those already in my collection have been drawn by my friend Roland Symons, I am most grateful to him not only for his meticulous drawings but for the patience and good humour with which he has born my ever-increasing requests for more.

Iain Swinnerton
January 2001

A studio portrait of a young officer wearing an officers' Sam Browne belt and sword sling. The cap and collar badges identify him as belonging to the Royal Wiltshire Yeomanry, but as his single pip of a 2nd Lt. is worn on the shoulder, this was probably taken after 1916 by which time the regiment had been dismounted and become the 6th (Wiltshire Yeomanry) Battalion, the Wiltshire Regiment.

1

CAP BADGES

The type of cap badge worn in the two world wars, and still being worn today, originated with the reorganisation of the army in 1881 and the introduction of county and other territorial affiliations for each regiment. Prior to this the principal feature of the helmet badge or plate had been the regimental number.

The introduction of the new undress cap for the ordinary soldiers of the infantry and some corps in 1874 resulted in a new type of badge, but although some regiments did adopt additional symbols for their badges, in the main the new badges still contained the old regimental number. These caps continued to be worn until 1895, but after the changes of 1881, the new type of cap badge with which we are familiar today came into common usage and by 1914, the start of the period covered by this book, they had become enshrined in army tradition.

Each badge has appeared with many minor variations over the years and in different materials, but the main features of the design have remained the same. They are drawn here in the simple outline style of the period and any fine details have been omitted for the sake of clarity and ease of identification.

The regiments are listed by arm of service in order of seniority – Regular Army Cavalry, Guards, Infantry and the Corps followed by the Territorial Force Yeomanry, the Territorial Force regiments, who had no regular army equivalent, the Territorial Force Battalions, who had their own badges, the London Regiment and the Cyclists Corps.

1st Life Guards

2nd Life Guards

Royal Horse Guards (The Blues)

Household Cavalry Composite
Regiment

The Household Battalion

Pre 1915   Post 1915
1st (King's) Dragoon Guards   2nd Dragoon Guards (Queen's Bays)

3rd (Prince of Wales's)   4th (Royal Irish) Dragoon Guards
Dragoon Guards

5th (Princess Charlotte of Wales's)   6th Dragoon Guards (Carabiniers)
Dragoon Guards

7th (Princess Royal's) Dragoon
Guards

1st (Royal) Dragoons

2nd Dragoons
(Royal Scots Greys)

3rd (King's Own) Hussars

4th (Queen's Own) Hussars

5th (Royal Irish Lancers)

6th (Inniskilling) Dragoons

7th (Queen's Own) Hussars

8th (King's Royal Irish) Hussars

9th (Queen's Royal) Lancers

10th (Prince of Wales's Own Royal) Hussars

11th (Prince Albert's Own) Lancers

12th (Prince of Wales's Royal) Lancers

13th Hussars

Pre 1915   Post 1915
14th (King's) Hussars

15th (The King's) Hussars

16th (The Queen's) Lancers

17th (Duke of Cambridge's Own)
Lancers

18th (Queen Mary's Own) Hussars

19th (Queen Alexandra's Own
Royal) Hussars

20th Hussars

21st (Empress of India's) Lancers

The Royal Flying Corps
'The Cavalry of the Air'

Grenadier Guards

Coldstream Guards

Scots Guards

Irish Guards

Welsh Guards
(raised 1915)

The Royal Scots (Lothian Regiment)

The Queen's (Royal West Surrey Regiment)

The Buffs (East Kent Regiment)

The King's Own
(Royal Lancaster Regiment)

The Northumberland Fusiliers

The Royal Warwickshire Regiment

The Royal Fusiliers
(City of London Regiment)

The King's (Liverpool Regiment)

The Norfolk Regiment

The Lincolnshire Regiment

The Devonshire Regiment

The Suffolk Regiment

Prince Albert's
(Somerset Light Infantry)

The Prince of Wales's Own
(West Yorkshire Regiment)

The East Yorkshire Regiment

The Bedfordshire Regiment

The Leicestershire Regiment

The Royal Irish Regiment

Alexandra, Princess of Wales's Own
(Yorkshire Regiment)

The Lancashire Fusiliers

The Royal Scots Fusiliers

The Cheshire Regiment

The Royal Welsh Fusiliers

The South Wales Borderers

The King's Own Scottish Borderers

The Cameronians (Scottish Rifles)

The Royal Inniskilling Fusiliers

The Gloucestershire Regiment

The Worcestershire Regiment

The East Lancashire Regiment

The East Surrey Regiment

The Duke of Cornwall's
Light Infantry

The Duke of Wellington's
(West Riding Regiment)

The Border Regiment

The Royal Sussex Regiment

The Hampshire Regiment

The South Staffordshire Regiment

The Dorsetshire Regiment

The Prince of Wales's Volunteers
(South Lancashire Regiment)

The Welsh Regiment

The Black Watch
(Royal Highlanders)

The Oxfordshire and Buckinghamshire
Light Infantry

The Essex Regiment

The Sherwood Foresters
(Nottinghamshire and Derbyshire) Regiment

The Loyal North Lancashire Regiment

The Northamptonshire Regiment

Princess Charlotte of Wales's
(Royal Berkshire Regiment)

The Queen's Own
(Royal West Kent Regiment)

The King's Own
(Yorkshire Light Infantry)

The King's
(Shropshire Light Infantry)

The Duke of Cambridge's Own
(Middlesex Regiment)

The King's Royal Rifle Corps

The Duke of Edinburgh's
(Wiltshire Regiment)

The Manchester Regiment

The Prince of Wales's
(North Staffordshire Regiment)

The York and Lancaster Regiment

The Durham Light Infantry

The Highland Light Infantry

Seaforth Highlanders
(Ross-Shire Buffs, The Duke of Albany's)

The Gordon Highlanders

The Queen's Own
Cameron Highlanders

The Royal Irish Rifles

Princess Victoria's
(Royal Irish Fusiliers)

The Connaught Rangers

Princess Louise's
(Argyll & Sutherland Highlanders)

The Prince of Wales's Leinster Regiment
(Royal Canadians)

The Royal Munster Fusiliers

The Royal Dublin Fusiliers

The Rifle Brigade
(The Prince Consort's Own)

The Royal Military College
Sandhurst

The Royal Military Academy
Woolwich

The General List

The Royal Regiment of Artillery

The Royal Horse Artillery   The Royal Field Artillery   The Royal Garrison Artillery

The Corps of Royal Engineers   The Army Service Corps

The Royal Army Medical Corps   The Army Veterinary Corps

The Army Chaplains' Department
(Christian)

The Army Chaplains' Department
(Jewish)

The Army Ordnance Department

The Army Pay Corps (Other Ranks)
*(Officers were drawn from the Army Pay
Department and wore the King's Crest of the
crowned lion)*

The Military Mounted Police

The Military Foot Police

The Army Remount Service

The School of Musketry   The Military Provost Staff Corps

The Army Gymnastic Staff   Army Scripture Readers

The Guards Machine Gun Company
(or Machine Gun Guards)

The Guards Machine Gun Regiment

20/21/22/23/29 &33rd Battalions
The Northumberland Fusiliers
(The Tyneside Scottish)

24/25/26/27/30 &34th Battalions
The Northumberland Fusiliers
(The Tyneside Irish)

14/15/16th Battalions
The Royal Warwickshire Regiment
(1st,2nd &3rd City of Birmingham)
(1st Battalion badge shown)

13th (Wandsworth) Battalion
The East Surrey Regiment

25th (Frontiersmen) Battalion
The Royal Fusiliers

38/39/40/41 & 42nd (Jewish) Battalions
The Royal Fusiliers

17/18/19 & 20th Battalions
The King's Liverpool Regiment
(The Liverpool Pals)

15th & 17th Battalions
The Prince of Wales's Own
(West Yorkshire Regiment)
(The Leeds Pals)

11th Lonsdale Battalion
The Border Regiment

18th (1st Public Works) Battalion (Pioneers)
The Duke of Cambridge's Own
(Middlesex Regiment)

16th Battalion
King's Royal Rifle Corps
(formed from Church Lads' Brigade Cadets)

14th (Young Citizen's) Battalion
The Royal Irish Rifles

Household Brigade
Officer Cadet Battalion

The Machine Gun Corps

The Motor Machine Gun Corps

The Tank Corps

The Forage Corps

The Labour Corps

The Imperial Camel Corps
(raised 1916)

Pre 1917

Post 1917

The Royal Defence Corps

With the exception of the Tank Corps, these units were all disbanded at the end of the war.

The Royal Wiltshire Yeomanry

The Warwickshire Yeomanry

The Yorkshire Hussars

The Nottinghamshire Hussars
(Sherwood Rangers)

The Staffordshire Yeomanry

The Shropshire Yeomanry

The Ayrshire Yeomanry
(Earl of Carrick's Own)

The Cheshire Yeomanry
(Earl of Chester's)

The Yorkshire Dragoons
(Queen's Own)

The Leicestershire Yeomanry
(Prince Albert's Own)

The North Somerset Yeomanry

The Duke of Lancaster's Own Yeomanry

The Lanarkshire Yeomanry

The Northumberland Hussars

The South Nottinghamshire Hussars

The Denbighshire Hussars

The Westmorland & Cumberland
Yeomanry

The Pembroke (Castle Martin)
Yeomanry

The Royal East Kent Yeomanry

The Hampshire Yeomanry
(Carabiniers)

The Royal Buckinghamshire Hussars

The Derbyshire Yeomanry

The Queen's Own Dorset Yeomanry

The Royal Gloucestershire Hussars

The Hertfordshire Yeomanry

The Berkshire (Hungerford) Yeomanry

The 1st County of London
(Middlesex, Duke of Cambridge's Hussars)

The Royal 1st Devon Yeomanry

The Duke of York's Own Loyal
Suffolk Hussars

The Royal North Devon Hussars

The Queen's Own Worcestershire Hussars

The Queen's Own West Kent
Yeomanry

The West Somerset Yeomanry

The Queen's Own
Oxfordshire Hussars

The Montgomeryshire Yeomanry

The Lothians & Border Horse

The Queen's Own Royal
Glasgow Yeomanry

The Lancashire Hussars

The Surrey Yeomanry
(Queen Mary's Regiment)

The Fife & Forfar Yeomanry

The Norfolk Yeomanry
(The King's Own Royal Regiment)

The Sussex Yeomanry

The Glamorgan Yeomanry

The Welsh Horse

The Lincolnshire Yeomanry

The City of London Yeomanry
(The Rough Riders)

The 2nd County of London Yeomanry
(Westminster Dragoons)

The 3rd County of London Yeomanry
(The Sharpshooters)

The Bedfordshire Yeomanry

The Essex Yeomanry

The Northamptonshire Yeomanry

The East Riding Yeomanry

The Lovat's Scouts

The Scottish Horse

The Special Reserve

The North Irish Horse

The South Irish Horse

1st King Edward's Horse

2nd King Edward's Horse

(The King's Overseas Dominions Regiment)

The Inns of Court Regiment

The Honourable Artillery Company
(Artillery)

The Honourable Artillery Company
(Infantry)

The Hertfordshire Regiment

The Monmouthshire Regiment

The Herefordshire Regiment

The Cambridgeshire Regiment

Most TF Infantry Battalions wore the badge of their parent Regular Army regiment but a few had their own cap badges.

8th Battalion
The King's Liverpool Regiment
(The Liverpool Irish)

10th Battalion
The King's Liverpool Regiment
(The Liverpool Scottish)

7th & 8th Battalions
The Prince of Wales's Own
(West Yorkshire Regiment)

The Brecknockshire Battalions
(1st, 2nd &3rd Territorial Battalions)
The South Wales Borderers

5th (Cinque Ports) Battalion
The Royal Sussex Regiment

6th (Duke of Connaught's Own) Battalion
The Hampshire Regiment

7th Battalion The Hampshire Regiment

8th Battalion The Hampshire Regiment
(The Princess Beatrice's Isle of Wight Rifles)

5th Battalion The Black Watch
(Royal Highlanders)
(formerly the Highland Cyclist Battalion)

The Buckinghamshire Battalion
The Oxfordshire & Buckinghamshire
Light Infantry

7th Robin Hood Battalion
The Sherwood Foresters
(Nottinghamshire Regiment)

4th (Territorial) Battalion
The Northamptonshire Regiment

7th Battalion
The Manchester Regiment

9th (Glasgow Highland) Battalion
The Highland Light Infantry

5th (Sutherland & Caithness) Battalion
The Seaforth Highlanders
(Ross-shire Buffs, The Duke of Albany's)

The Royal Monmouthshire
Royal Engineers

Royal Jersey Militia
(later 7th (Service) Battalion
Royal Irish Rifles)

Royal Guernsey Light Infantry
(later 6th (Service) Battalion
Royal Irish Regiment)

The cap badge identifies this young soldier as a Private of the King's
Liverpool Regiment. He is wearing 1914 pattern leather equipment.

When the Territorial Force was formed from the Yeomanry and Volunteers in 1907, volunteer rifle regiments and corps were converted to volunteer battalions of their regular army county regiments. However, the London area volunteer battalions, having no regular army equivalent, were excluded from the system and joined together to form a completely new regiment which was designated in the Army List as The London Regiment.

It was to consist of 28 battalions, but the Honourable Artillery Company, founded in 1537, which was numbered 26 and the Inns of Court Rifle Volunteers, founded in 1584, numbered 27, did not join (it is said they were dissatisfied with their low precedence as they were the two senior regiments). These two numbers were left vacant and there were only actually 26 battalions. The HAC continued in its dual artillery and infantry role being mainly an officer-producing unit and the Inns of Court regiment also became an officer-training corps.

1ˢᵗ, 2ⁿᵈ, 3ʳᵈ & 4ᵗʰ City of London Battalion
(The Royal Fusiliers)

5ᵗʰ City of London Battalion
(The London Rifle Brigade)

6ᵗʰ City of London Battalion
(City of London Rifles)

7ᵗʰ City of London Battalion

8th City of London Battalion
(The Post Office Rifles)

9th County of London Battalion
(Queen Victoria's)

10th County of London Battalion
(Hackney)

11th County of London Battalion
(Finsbury Rifles)

12th County of London Battalion
(The Rangers)

13th County of London Battalion
(Kensington)

14th County of London Battalion
(The London Scottish)

15th County of London Battalion
(Prince of Wales's Own Civil Service Rifles)

16th County of London Battalion
(Queen's Westminster Rifles)

17th County of London Battalion
(Poplar & Stepney Rifles)

18th County of London Battalion
(London Irish Rifles)

19th County of London Battalion
(St.Pancras)

20th County of London Battalion
(Blackheath & Woolwich)

21st County of London Battalion
(First Surrey Rifles)

22nd & 24th County of London Battalions
(The Queen's)

23rd County of London Battalion

25th County of London (Cyclist) Battalion

28th County of London Battalion
(Artists Rifles)

A number of volunteer regiments had cyclist sections prior to the formation of the Territorial Force in 1908, but the only regiment to consist solely of cyclists was the 26th Middlesex Cyclist Volunteers who, on the formation of the TF, became the 25th County of London Battalion, the London Regiment (see previous page). Nine other cyclist battalions were formed at that time, by 1914 a further 5 had been formed and the Army Cyclist Corps was formed on the 7th November 1914.

The Army Cyclist Corps

1st/1st London Divisional Cyclist Company

The Cyclist Battalions

Highland

Northern

Kent

Huntingdonshire

Essex & Suffolk

9th Hampshire

The cap badge is very indistinct, but the collar badges clearly identify this Corporal as a member of the East Riding Yeomanry.

2

COLLAR BADGES

Metal collar badges were introduced for all regiments of infantry for the first time in 1874, following the introduction of a universal pattern button and the abolition of individual regimental patterns as an economy measure. The exceptions were the three regiments of Foot Guards, who already wore embroidered cloth collar badges, and the 60th Foot (The Kings Royal Rifle Corps) and Rifle Brigade for whom no badges were authorised. At first they were only worn by other ranks i.e. ordinary soldiers and non-commissioned officers.

After the reorganisation of the army in 1881, officers began to wear their badges of rank on their shoulder cords (previously they had worn them on their collars) and from then on they also wore collar badges.

The Cavalry, Royal Regiment of Artillery (although their NCOs had long worn brass gun collar badges), Royal Engineers and Army Service Corps eventually followed suit, and by the outbreak of World War One, the whole of the army was wearing some form of badge on the collars of at least one of their orders of dress.

Many were very similar to, or actually smaller versions of, the cap badge and those are not reproduced here. Only those that are radically different are included in this section, if they are not found here, the reader should consult the cap badges in Chapter 1.

The shortened titles of the regiments normally used are given in this chapter; for the full designations refer to Chapter 1.

The Berkshire Yeomanry

1ˢᵗ Dragoon Guards

The Royal Dragoons

Royal Irish Lancers

14ᵗʰ Hussars

15ᵗʰ Hussars

21ˢᵗ Lancers

The Scots Guards

The Irish Guards

The Royal Scots

The Royal Irish Regiment

The Devonshire Regiment

The Suffolk Regiment

The Lancashire Fusiliers

The East Lancashire Regiment

The East Surrey Regiment

The Royal Irish Fusiliers

The Royal Scots Fusiliers

The Cheshire Regiment

The King's Own Scottish Borderers

The Duke of Cornwall's
Light Infantry

The Duke of Wellington's Regiment

The Royal Sussex Regiment

The Hampshire Regiment

The Dorsetshire Regiment

The Black Watch

The Essex Regiment

The Loyal North Lancashire Regiment

The Northamptonshire Regiment

The Royal West Kent Regiment

The Manchester Regiment

The Seaforth Highlanders

The Gordon Highlanders

The Cameron Highlanders

The Argyll & Sutherland Highlanders

The Connaught Rangers

16th (Cardiff City) Battalion
The Welsh Regiment
(The Cardiff Pals)

The Royal Regiment of Artillery
(Officers)

The Corps of Royal Engineers
(Officers)

The Army Pay Corps

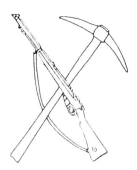

Pioneer Battalions
of Infantry Regiments

The Staffordshire Yeomanry

The Dorset Yeomanry

Devon Yeomanry

North Devon Yeomanry

The Oxfordshire Hussars

The Glasgow Yeomanry

The Norfolk Yeomanry

The Glamorgan Yeomanry

The Rough Riders

The City of London Yeomanry

Inns of Court Regiment

Private John Burgess of the Duke of Cornwall's Light Infantry as shown by his cap badge and shoulder titles. His collar badges show that he was a member of the Pioneer Battalion.

Sgt Reginald Vincent of the Royal Army Service Corps. The shoulder title of RASC dates the photograph to 1919 or later when the Corps was awarded the title Royal for its services during the war. This is substantiated by the 5 overseas stripes which were not instituted until 1918. He is also wearing the ribbon of the 1914 Star first awarded in 1917.

3

BADGES OF RANK

The British Army went to war in 1914 wearing, in most cases, the same badges of rank that were instituted during the reorganisation of the army in 1881. The whole subject of rank badges is most complex: all that can be done in a book of this nature is to try and give an example of the most common, as it is quite impossible to deal with all the regimental variations. Two new sets of regulations were introduced during the war; the first in 1915 with the end of the first phase of the war and the introduction of the New Armies and the second in 1920 at the end of the war on the reorganisation of the peace time army.

The problem is that in many cases these were ignored during the war and all ranks continued to wear the old badges until the uniform was replaced. Consequently, it is possible to find photographs with badges of rank some years out of date which makes dating difficult.

Officers' rank badges up to the rank of Colonel consisted of a combination of crowns and stars (pips) which were originally worn on the collar, but for full and ceremonial dress these were moved to the shoulder cords in 1880. With the introduction of khaki service dress in 1902, a new system of cuff badges was adopted with the same crowns and pips but on a background of rings of braid, which roughly corresponded to the equivalent rank cuff rings of the Royal Navy.

In the trenches these proved to be difficult to recognise and many officers changed to wearing them on the shoulder straps, although this met with strong disapproval from the authorities back at home. However, common sense prevailed in the end and from 1917 it was permissible to wear either and cuff badges were officially abolished in 1920.

Non commissioned officers' badges of rank were a combination of crowns and chevrons (stripes) which were worn on the arm either above or below the elbow depending on the rank as a general rule the more senior the rank, the lower down the arm. In dealing with NCOs' badges, it is necessary always to remember the distinction between a rank and an appointment.

The Sergeant Major we know today, for instance, is first mentioned as an appointment in 1724, but he was, in fact, the senior sergeant of the Colonel's Company and although he had been referred to as Sgt Major since 1680, was only classed as a Staff Sergeant. The rank of Sergeant Major was not officially established until 1797. In 1802 it was laid down that Sergeant Majors should wear, point down, four chevrons (commonly called stripes) of silver lace edged with blue. Later, a crown was added to the four bars and this was still being worn by some regiments as late as 1915. Eventually the magnificent badge of the Royal Arms that they wear today was introduced. Sergeant Majors of the Guards had always worn this superimposed on their stripes.

The term Warrant Officer came in with the great reorganisation of the army in 1881 when Sergeant Majors and Bandmasters became Warrant Officers, so called because they received a warrant just as officers received a commission. At the outbreak of war there were over 20 senior NCO appointments ranking as Warrant Officers including Regimental Sergeant Majors, Conductors in the Army Ordnance Department and Master Gunners in the Royal Regiment of Artillery to name just three. The Army Order 70 of 1915 divided them into two classes, Warrant Officers Class I and II. The latter included Company Sergeant Majors of the Infantry, Battery Sergeant Majors of the Artillery and Troop Sergeant Majors in the Cavalry.

Sergeants have worn three chevrons as their badge of rank since 1802. To the original rank have been added Armourer Sgt (1811), Hospital Sgt (1824), Farrier Sergeant (1852), Quartermaster Sgt (1856), Sgt Instructor of Musketry (1860), Sgt Cook (1862), Pioneer Sgt, the only man in the British Army to still wear a beard (1872), Orderly Room Sgt (1881) and Band Sgt (1900). Each wore a special badge above his stripes to denote his qualification, as will be seen in the illustrations, as does a Recruiting Sgt, who wears crossed Union Flags and a crown. Sergeants in Cavalry Regiments have always worn distinctive regimental badges above their stripes.

Colour Sergeants were introduced in 1813, these were very senior sergeants whose duty was to guard the colours in action, and it is an honoured rank. At first they wore a single chevron with a crown, flag and crossed swords above their stripes and a scarlet sash over their shoulder, but later they used the normal three stripes of a sergeant with the crown and flags. There were also Lance Sergeants, a rank now only used in the Guards

Regiments. This was an appointment: they were corporals who were qualified to be sergeants and were waiting for a vacancy.

Corporals since 1802 have worn two chevrons. It is often assumed that Bombardier is the Royal Artillery term for a corporal. This is true today, but the Artillery used to have both — Corporals wore two stripes as the rest of the army, Bombardiers, who served the guns, wore one. The rank of Corporal in the Royal Regiment of Artillery was abolished in 1915, and all the Bombardiers then put up two stripes.

Just as there were Lance Sergeants there were also Lance Corporals who wore a single stripe and, after the abolition of Corporal in the Artillery, Lance Bombardiers who also wore just one stripe.

Until the distinction was abolished by Royal Warrant in 1872, ranks in the Guards were one above those in the rest of the army a corporal in the Guards, for example, ranked as a sergeant in the infantry of the line. Just to be confusing, the Household Cavalry to this day commemorate this distinction and refer to their sergeants as Corporals of Horse and their Sergeant Majors as Corporal Majors.

Before 1915
Worn on the upper arm

Lance Corporal
Bombardier (Royal Artillery)

Corporal

Sergeant

Colour Sergeant
Rifle Regiment

Colour Sergeant
Line Infantry

1st Class Staff Sergeant
(appointments such as Company
or Troop Sgt Major, Company
Quartermaster Sgt, Paymaster Sgt
and Orderly Room Sgt)

Worn on the cuff

Regimental Quartermaster Sergeant

Quartermaster Sergeant
Royal Artillery

Quartermaster Corporal Major
(Household Cavalry)

Bandmaster

Regimental Sergeant Maior
Conductor of Ordnance

Master Gunner 1st Class
Royal Artillery

Worn on the upper arm

Sgt Major Instructor
Musketry

Sgt Major Instructor
Signals

Sgt Major Instructor
Gymnastics

Recruiting Sgt.

Sgt Drummer

Sgt Bugler

Sgt Trumpeter

Sgt Instructor Signals

Sgt Instructor Musketry

Sgt Instructor Gymnastics

Sgt Instructor Gunnery

Riding Instructor
Rough Rider
Remount Trainer

Pioneer Sgt

Farrier Sgt

Armourer Sgt

Pipe Sgt
Scottish Regiments

Pipe Sgt
Irish Regiments

Flight Sgt
Royal Flying Corps

Worn on the cuff

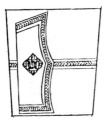

Second Lieutenant

Lieutenant

Captain

Major

Lieutenant Colonel

Colonel

Scottish Regiments - worn on the cuff

Second Lieutenant

Lieutenant

Captain

Major

Lieutenant Colonel

Colonel

Worn on the shoulder straps

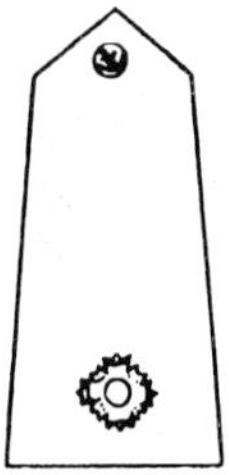

Second Lieutenant

Lieutenant

Captain

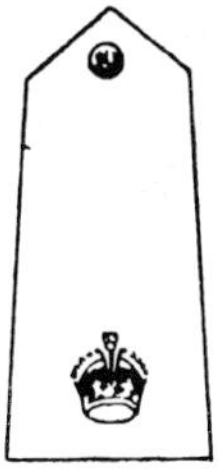

Major

Lieutenant Colonel

Colonel

Brigadier General

Major General

Lieutenant General

General

Field Marshal

Staff Officers Collar Gorget

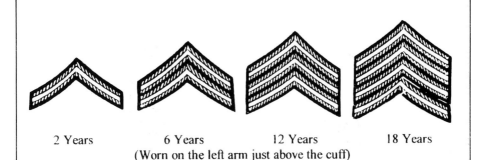

2 Years   6 Years   12 Years   18 Years

(Worn on the left arm just above the cuff)

Overseas Service Stripes 1914-18
(Blue – not issued until 1918, worn on the right arm just above the cuff)
(If the bottom one is red which will show up as slightly darker on a black and white
photograph, it indicates that the soldier went overseas before 31st December 1914)

Wound Stripes – introduced in August 1916.
(Gold – one for each time the man was wounded, worn on the left cuff)

4

TRADE AND PROFICIENCY BADGES

Badges to denote a soldier's proficiency in the skilled use of his weapons or his expertise at a particular trade have been in use since the middle of the 19th century. It was in that period that a series of competitions designed to generally improve the ordinary soldier's skill in shooting, swordsmanship and use of the lance for cavalrymen were introduced.

In addition there were tests in riding and driving because, of course, the horse was the main means of transport for the whole army and even the infantry used horse drawn wagons for carrying their supplies, mobile cookhouses and wounded.

At first many of these badges were awarded as prizes, often accompanied by a cash reward with competitions being held at regular intervals when previous winners had to re-qualify. Gradually, the prize aspect was dropped and they became straight-forward skill-at-arms badges which were much prized.

Although some of those peculiar to the old Volunteer Force were discontinued on the formation of the Territorial Force in 1908, many survived and were worn by soldiers of the 1914-18 War alongside those worn for many years by the Regular Army.

Sgt Major Instructor in Gunnery

Trade Badges

Smith/Armourer

Saddler
Saddle Tree/Collar/Harness Maker

Farrier

Wheelwright

Pioneer

Medical Orderly
RAMC

Bandsman

Pilot
Royal Flying Corps

Air Observer
Royal Flying Corps

Skill at Arms Badges

Marksman

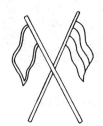

Signaller

Distance Judging

Army Scout

1st Class Army Scout

Scout
(Regiments from India)

Infantry Bomber

Trench Mortar Gunner

Range Taker

Machine Gunner   Lewis Gunner   Hotchkiss Gunner

All the preceding skill at arms badges could be worn with crowns or stars to denote varying degrees of skill as shown in these examples.

Territorial Force Efficiency Badges

Good Shooting   One years service   Five years service

Appointment Badges

Gun Layer

Stretcher Bearer

Observer

Trained Soldier
(Guards Brigade only)

Bugler

Bugler
(Rifle Regiments)

Drummer

Trumpeter

Bandsman

Qualified Instructor
Field Engineering (RE)

Interpreter

Best RA Battery Prize
(Worn by all NCOs and men in the Battery)

Individual Best Gunner Prize

Skill at Driving

Best Swordsman

Best with Lance

All these badges may also be seen with crowns or stars above denoting the prize class.

5

REGIMENTAL ARM BADGES

The wearing of distinctive badges by Sergeants and, in the Cavalry, sometimes also by Corporals either on or above their chevrons seems to have originated with H.R.H.The Duke of Cumberland who in 1801, as Colonel of the 15th King's Light Dragoons, asked permission for his regiment's NCOs to wear a Royal Crown above their chevrons.

By the beginning of World War I, the senior NCOs of all cavalry regiments (including the Yeomanry) were wearing distinctive regimental arm badges mostly in silver. In most cases, these were the same as the cap badges, but a few were completely different and those are the ones that are reproduced here.

Sergeants of the Royal Regiment of Artillery wore a brass gun above their chevrons from the later 19th century, and Sergeants of the Royal Engineers similarly wore a grenade.

In the case of the Army Medical Department, however, the arm badge of the Geneva Cross was worn by all ranks.

The sergeants of the regiments of the Brigade of Guards had worn distinctive arm badges for many years before World War I and this tradition was continued on the formation of the Welsh Guards in 1915, their sergeants being given the Red Dragon of Wales.

Possibly unique is the Eagle of the Essex Regiment, which appears to have been worn on occasions both as an arm badge and also as a collar badge, but in the latter case only by officers on their ceremonial dress and mess kit. This commemorated the capture of the Regimental Eagle (the equivalent to a British Regimental Flag) of the French 62nd Regiment at Salamanca in the Peninsular War.

The Essex Regiment's Eagle Badge

5th Dragoon Guards   5th (Royal Irish) Lancers   7th Hussars

9th Lancers   12th Lancers   19th Hussars

21st Lancers   Inns of Court Regiment

The Nottinghamshire
Hussars

The Staffordshire Yeomanry

The Shropshire Yeomanry

Duke of Lancaster's Own
Yeomanry

Queen's Own
Royal Glasgow Yeomanry

The Lancashire Hussars

The Norfolk Yeomanry

City of London Yeomanry
(Rough Riders)

3rd County of London
Yeomanry
(Sharpshooters)

Grenadier Guards   Coldstream Guards   Scots Guards

Irish Guards   Welsh Guards

The Cameronians
(Piper's Badge)

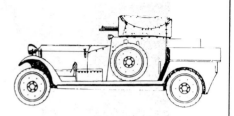

Army Service Corps Armoured Car Companies

Light Armoured Motor Batteries

Armoured Car Companies

Sgt Royal Artillery

Sgt Royal Engineers

Sgt Royal Army Medical Corps

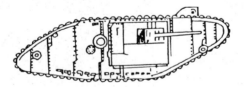

The Tank Corps

A Sergeant Gymnastics Instructor in the Grenadier Guards as shown by his shoulder titles, the buttons down the front of his tunic worn singly and the Guards-type cap. He has two overseas service stripes denoting that he has served at least a year and a day out of the country.

6

SHOULDER TITLES

Badges worn on the shoulder straps to identify the bearer's regiment were another result of the reorganisation of the army in 1881. They were first introduced for officer's tropical uniforms, but after the issue of khaki drill uniforms in India in 1885 were thereafter worn by all ranks. By 1914 they were of metal with the exception of the Brigade of Guards who wore embroidered cloth titles.

Ray Westlake in his authoritative book on the subject (see Bibliography) lists 1858 examples, but as most are very easily identifiable, only a few representative examples are shown here.

21st Hussars

Shropshire Yeomanry

**24th-27th Northumberland
Fusiliers (Tyneside Irish)**

**London Territorial
Ambulances RAMC**

Royal Field Artillery

**1st Brigade (City of London)
Territorial RFA**

Royal Engineers

RE Signal Service

RE Railway Companies

Duke of Cornwall's
Light Infantry

Northumberland Fusiliers

East Kent Regiment

3rd Volunteer Battalion
Royal Warwickshire Regiment

14th Battalion London Regiment

Tank Corps

Royal Flying Corps

Suffolk Yeomanry

Company Quartermaster Sergeant Donald Hopping of the 14th London Regiment (The London Scottish) wearing a South Africa Medal with two bars, the three WWI Medals and the Territorial Force Efficiency Medal.

7

MEDALS

The first medal to be issued was the **1914 Star,** often wrongly called the **Mons Star.** This was awarded to all officers and men of the British Expeditionary Force who had served in France or Belgium between the 5th of August and the 22nd November, 1914.

Members of the Indian Expeditionary Force were also eligible for the award, as were civilian doctors, nurses and others employed in military hospitals and officers and men of the Royal Navy, Royal Naval Reserve (RNR), Royal Naval Volunteer Reserve (RNVR) and Royal Marines who served ashore in a Theatre of War (basically those at Antwerp), but not those on ships afloat. The medal is made of bronze and was authorised in 1917; it hangs from a red, white and blue ribbon of watered silk. The reverse of the medal is plain and bears the number, rank, name and unit of the recipient.

In 1919, King George V approved the issue of a bar to those who had already been awarded the 1914 Star and had actually served under the fire of the enemy in France or Belgium between those dates. This was signified on the ribbon by a small silver rosette.

In the same year, the King sanctioned another version of the medal known as the **1914-15 Star.** The shape and size are identical, but in the centre the words Aug and Nov have been removed and 1914 has been replaced by 1914-15. The ribbon was the same. This was awarded to all personnel who had served in a Theatre of War, and this time members of the Royal Navy, Royal Naval Air Service, Royal Naval Reserve, Royal Naval Volunteer Reserve, Dominion Naval Forces and Royal Marines who served at sea or ashore in a Theatre of War were eligible as well as men of the Merchant Navy and canteen staff who had served in a ship of war at sea. Men who already had the 1914 Star, with or without the bar were not eligible.

The second medal was the silver **British War Medal,** approved in 1919, which commemorated the end of the war and was later extended to 1920 to cover the post-war mine clearance at sea and the campaigns in Russia and the Baltic, Black and Caspian Seas. The front of the medal has a portrait of the King with the inscription *GEORGIUS V: BRITT: OMN: REX et IND: IMP.* The other side depicts St.George on his horse, under a sun of victory, trampling underfoot the eagle device of the enemy (known collectively as the Central Powers) with a skull and crossbones to represent Death. The ribbon is of orange silk with a blue edging and a black and white stripe down each side. The number, rank and name of the recipient are engraved around the rim.

The third medal was the **Victory Medal**. Made of bronze, on the front it has a winged figure of Victory and on the back the words *The Great War for Civilisation*. An oak leaf was authorised to be worn on the ribbon if a man had been Mentioned in Despatches: only one was worn however many times the man was mentioned. The ribbon was red with green and violet on either side shaded to form two rainbows. The conditions for eligibility were much the same as for the War Medal. The number, rank and name of the holder were, as in the War Medal, engraved around the rim.

Many people have been disappointed to find that their ancestor was not awarded any medals although they did serve in WWI. This is because they did not serve in an actual Theatre of War - there was no equivalent of the WW2 Defence Medal for the First World War.

These last two medals were also awarded to members of the Royal Air Force, formed in April 1918 by the merging of the Royal Flying Corps and The Royal Naval Air Service. A scheme to issue Campaign Bars for the War Medal as had been done in the South African War was proposed: the bars for the navy were actually published in Admiralty Orders, but they were never issued to any of the services on the grounds of cost. Medals for men who were killed or died in service were issued to the next-of-kin

The other medal issued to commemorate service in WWI is the **Territorial Force War Medal**, issued to all members of the Territorial Force (including Nursing Sisters) who were in the TF on the 4th August 1914 and to former Territorials who had completed 4 years service if they had re-joined on or before 30th September 1914, but they had to have undertaken to serve outside the United Kingdom on or before the 30th September 1914 or to have done so between 4th August and the 12th November 1914.

The medal is bronze with the head of the King on the face: on the reverse are the words *For Voluntary Service Overseas 1914-19* and round the rim *Territorial War Medal.* The ribbon is watered yellow with two green stripes and the medal will be named round the rim with the number, rank and name of the recipient.

There were also, of course, the medals for Gallantry and Distinguished Service and you may well also see the ribbons of the South African War and other pre-war campaigns being worn by regular or former regular soldiers.

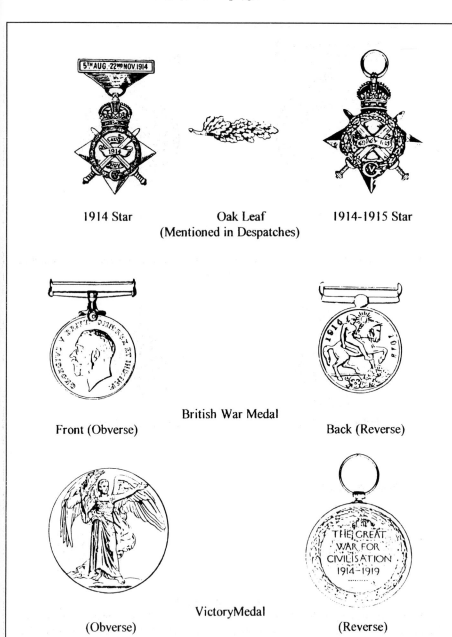

1914 Star

Oak Leaf
(Mentioned in Despatches)

1914-1915 Star

British War Medal

Front (Obverse)

Back (Reverse)

VictoryMedal

(Obverse)

(Reverse)

Obverse   Reverse

Territorial Force War Medal

Other medals which pre–war regular soldiers and reservists recalled to the colours may be seen wearing.

India Medal 1895   Ashanti Star 1896

South African Medal

Queen Victoria's (1899-1900)   King Edward's (1901-2)

The obverse bears the head of the sovereign at the time, the Reverse is the same for both medals.

Central Africa Medal
1891-8

Sudan Medal
1896-7

East & Central Africa Medal
1897-9

China Medal
1900

Ashanti Medal
1901

Africa General Service
1902

Tibet Medal 1903-4

Indian General Service Medal 1908

The Victoria Cross

The Distinguished Service Order

The Distinguished Conduct
Medal

The Military Cross

The Military Medal

The Order of the British Empire
(Instituted 1917)

The British Empire Medal

8

MISCELLANEOUS

Many regiments had old customs that were perpetuated in an item of dress enabling the regiment of the person in the photograph to be established. A few examples are:

The Gloucestershire Regiment wore an additional badge at the back of their caps or helmets to commemorate their back-to-back stand against the French Cavalry at the Battle of Alexandria on the 21st of March, 1801.

The Royal Welsh Fusiliers wore a black flash (a knot of black ribbons) on the back of the collar representing the patch of black leather which protected the tunic from the grease and powder with which the soldiers were obliged to dress their pigtails. The regiment embarked for Barbados in January 1808 and then went to Canada so never received the order abolishing the pigtail in 1808: the flash commemorates the fact that they were the last soldiers to wear the pigtail.

The Light Infantry, Rifle Brigade and Kings Royal Rifle Corps all wear black buttons and badges and green or black chevrons, which will show up on a photograph in contrast to the usual brass worn by the rest of the army.

A photograph of a soldier saluting bare-headed indicates he was a member of the Blues (the Royal Horse Guards) who are allowed to do this to commemorate their Colonel and commander of all the cavalry at the Battle of Warburg in 1760, the Marquis of Granby. He led the charge and lost both his hat and his wig, revealing his bald pate, which is the origin of the phrase "going at something bald-headed".

A photograph of a soldier wearing a white lanyard on his right shoulder instead of on the customary left usually indicates a Gunner of the Royal Horse Artillery, commemorating their traditional post on the Right of the Line.

The Guards Regiments may be distinguished by the arrangements of the buttons down the front of their tunics. The Grenadiers wear them singly, the Coldstream Guards in pairs , the Scots in threes, the Irish in fours and the Welsh in groups of five.

Badges of the Women's Services and various other supporting organisations are shown on the following pages.

IMPERIAL SERVICE

Imperial Service Tablet
(Worn by Territorials who
volunteered from 1912 for
overseas service). Worn on
<u>Right</u> breast.

The Corps of Military
Accountants
(1919)

The Volunteer Training Corps
(The Home Guard of WWI)

First Class Shot

Marksman

Signaller

Ambulance Section

The Women's Services

Queen Alexandra's Imperial Military
Nursing Service

Queen Alexandra's Imperial Military
Nursing Service Reserve

First Aid Nursing Yeomanry
(FANY)

Women's Legion

Women's Army Auxiliary Corps
(renamed Queen Mary's Army Auxiliary Corps in 1919)

Extra Regimentally Employed List

Motor Volunteer Companies

National Motor Volunteers

Army Motor Reserve

BIBLIOGRAPHY

Head-Dress Badges of the British Army Vol.1 Up to the end of the Great War
Arthur L.Kipling and Hugh L.King. 2nd Revised Edition reprinted 1978.
Muller, Blond and White. London.

Military Badges of the British Empire 1914-18.
Reginald H.W.Cox. 1983.
The Standard Art Book Co. Chicago. Illinois.

Badges of the British Army 1820 to the Present.
F.Wilkinson. 9th Edition 1997, reprinted 1998.
Arms and Armour Press. London.

Military Badge Collecting.
John Gaylor. 6th Edition 1996, reprinted 1997.
Leo Cooper (Pen & Sword Books Ltd.) Barnsley, Yorks

British Army Collar Badges 1881 to the Present.
Colin Churchill and Ray Westlake. 1986.
Arms and Armour Press. London

Collecting Metal Shoulder Titles.
Ray Westlake. 1996.
Leo Cooper (Pen & Sword Books Ltd.) Barnsley, Yorks.

British Army Proficiency Badges
Denis Edwards and David Langley. 1984
Wardley Publishing, Prestatyn.

British Battles and Medals.
E.C.Joslin, A.R.Litherland and B.T.Simpkin. 1988
Spink and Son Ltd., London.

Clothing Regulations 1914.
(Facsimile edition of *Regulations for the Clothing of the Army:
Part 1. The Regular Army.* War Office 1914.)
Ray Westlake Military Books.

World War One British Army.
Brassey's History of Uniforms Series.
Stephen Bull 1998.
Brasseys (UK) Ltd. London

Osprey's Men-at-Arms Series
No.81 *The British Army 1914-18*
No.182 *British Battle Insignia 1. 1914-18*
No.245 *British Territorial Units 1914-18*

Osprey's Elite Series
No.24 *The Old Contemptibles*

Osprey's Warrior Series
No.16 *British Tommy 1914-18.*

Osprey Publishing, Wellingborough, Northants.

General Reading.

World War One Army Ancestry.
Norman Holding. 3rd Edition 1997
Federation of Family History Societies.

The Location of British Army Records 1914-1918
Norman Holding and Iain Swinnerton. 4th Edition 1999
Federation of Family History Societies.

More Sources of World War I Ancestry.
Norman Holding. 3rd Edition 1998.
Federation of Family History Societies.

An Introduction to the British Army: its history, traditions and records.
Iain Swinnerton. 1996 reprinted 1998.
Federation of Family History Societies.

British Regiments 1914-18
Brigadier E.A.James OBE.TD. 4th Edition 1994
Naval & Military Press, London

The World War One Source Book.
Philip J.Heythornthwaite. 1992, reprinted 1994.
Arms & Armour Press, London.

The British Army of 1914-18

Total number of infantry battalions of all types per regiment.

Grenadier Guards	5
Coldstream Guards	5
Scots Guards	3
Irish Guards	3
Welsh Guards	2
Royal Scots	34
Queen's Royal West Surrey Regiment	27
East Kent Regiment	15
King's Own Royal Lancaster Regiment	17
Northumberland Fusiliers	51
Royal Warwickshire Regiment	30
Royal Fusiliers	47
King's Liverpool Regiment	49
Norfolk Regiment	19
Lincolnshire Regiment	19
Devonshire Regiment	29
Suffolk Regiment	23
Somerset Light Infantry	18
West Yorkshire Regiment	35
East Yorkshire Regiment	19
Bedfordshire Regiment	21
Leicestershire Regiment	22
Royal Irish Regiment	10
Princess of Wales's Yorkshire Regiment	24
Lancashire Fusiliers	31
Royal Scots Fusiliers	18
Cheshire Regiment	38
Royal Welsh Fusiliers	40
South Wales Borderers	21
King's Own Scottish Borderers	14
Cameronians	27
Royal Inniskilling Fusiliers	13
Gloucestershire Regiment	24
Worcestershire Regiment	22
East Lancashire Regiment	17
East Surrey Regiment	18
Duke of Cornwall's Light Infantry	15
Duke of Wellington's West Riding Regiment	22
Border Regiment	16

Royal Sussex Regiment	26
Hampshire Regiment	32
South Staffordshire Regiment	17
Dorsetshire Regiment	11
South Lancashire Regiment	21
Welsh Regiment	35
Black Watch	22
Oxfordshire & Buckinghamshire Light Infantry	18
Essex Regiment	30
Sherwood Foresters	33
Loyal North Lancashire Regiment	21
Northamptonshire Regiment	13
Royal Berkshire Regiment	16
Royal West Kent Regiment	18
King's Own Yorkshire Light Infantry	24
King's Shropshire Light Infantry	12
Middlesex Regiment	49
King's Royal Rifle Corps	28
Wiltshire Regiment	10
Manchester Regiment	44
North Staffordshire Regiment	19
York and Lancaster Regiment	22
Durham Light Infantry	42
Highland Light Infantry	33
Seaforth Highlanders	17
Gordon Highlanders	23
Cameron Highlanders	14
Royal Irish Rifles	21
Royal Irish Fusiliers	14
Connaught Rangers	6
Argyll & Sutherland Highlanders	26
Leinster Regiment	7
Royal Munster Fusiliers	11
Royal Dublin Fusiliers	11
Rifle Brigade	28
Honourable Artillery Company	3
Hertfordshire Regiment	4
Monmouthshire Regiment	10
Herefordshire Regiment	3
Cambridgeshire Regiment	4
London Regiment	88
Northern Cyclist Battalion	3
Highland Cyclist Battalion	3
Kent Cyclist Battalion	3
Huntingdonshire Cyclist Battalion	3

ROYAL WARRANT.

XIX.—Warrant Officers, Class II.

GEORGE R.I.

WHEREAS WE deem it expedient to introduce in Our Regular Army, Special Reserve and Territorial Force a new rank of Warrant Officer, below that now existing and to provide for the inclusion therein of certain senior non-commissioned officers ;

IT IS OUR WILL AND PLEASURE that such a rank shall be created accordingly, to be designated Warrant Officers, Class II. ;

Class II. shall consist of the following ranks and appointments :—

Master gunner, 3rd Class.
Army schoolmaster (when not a Warrant Officer, Class I.).
Garrison quartermaster-serjeant.
Quartermaster - corporal - major   (Household Cavalry).

Regimental quartermaster-serjeant.
Squadron-corporal-major (Household Cavalry).
Squadron-serjeant-major.
Battery-serjeant-major.
Troop-serjeant-major.
Company-serjeant-major.

The rates of pay of warrant officers, Class II., shall be those severally prescribed for the above ranks and appointments.

OUR FURTHER WILL AND PLEASURE with regard to pensions and allowances of Warrant Officers, Class II., will be made known at a later date.

IT IS ALSO OUR WILL AND PLEASURE that all warrant officers serving as such prior to the date of this Our Warrant shall form Class I., and wherever the words Warrant Officer occur in existing Warrants or Regulations they shall be read as meaning Warrant Officer, Class I.

Given at Our Court at St. James's, this 28th day of January, 1915, in the 5th year of Our Reign.

By His Majesty's Command,

Army Council's Instructions.   KITCHENER.

(1.) Promotions to warrant officer, Class I., will be open as hitherto to all non-commissioned officers of the rank of serjeant and upwards, as well as to warrant officers, Class II.

(2.) Non-commissioned officers now holding the rank or appointment of quartermaster-serjeant, or squadron-, battery-, troop- or company-serjeant-major and quartermaster-serjeant, will, for the purposes of promotion to warrant officer, Class I., retain their existing seniority on promotion lists.

A.O. 174. **Badges of Rank, Warrant Officers.**—With
1915. reference to Army Order 70 of 1915, the following
badges of rank will be worn by the Warrant Officers
specified :—

WARRANT OFFICERS—CLASS I.

Conductor, A.O.C.	Crown and Wreath.
1st Class Staff-Serjeant-Major, A.S.C. and A.P.C.	Crown and Wreath.
Master Gunner, 1st Class ...	Crown and Wreath and Gun.
Schoolmaster, 1st Class... ...	Crown and Wreath.
Sub-Conductor, A.O.C.... ...	Royal Arms.
Master Gunner, 2nd Class ...	Royal Arms and Gun.
Garrison Serjeant-Major ...	
Schoolmaster	Royal Arms.
Serjeant-Major	
Farrier-Corporal-Major... ...	Royal Arms and
Farrier-Serjeant-Major	Horseshoe.
Serjeant-Major, R.A.M.C. ...	Royal Arms and Geneva Cross.
Serjeant-Major, Gymnastic Staff	Royal Arms and crossed swords.
Serjeant-Major, School of Musketry ...	Royal Arms and crossed rifles.
Bandmaster	Special badge, except Household Cavalry and Foot Guards.

WARRANT OFFICERS—CLASS II.

Master Gunner, 3rd Class ...	Crown and Gun.
Schoolmaster	Crown.
Garrison Quartermaster-Serjeant	
Quartermaster-Corporal-Major ...	
*Regimental Quartermaster-Serjeant...	
Squadron Corporal-Major ...	Crown.
Squadron Serjeant-Major ...	
Battery Serjeant-Major	
Troop Serjeant-Major	
Company Serjeant-Major	

* The regimental Quartermaster-Serjeant, School of Musketry
wears crossed rifles in addition, and the regimental Quartermaster-Serjeant. R.A.M.C., a Geneva Cross.

All the above badges are worn below the elbow.

THE JERVIS WORLD WAR I
PHOTOGRAPHIC INDEX

The aim of this index is to ensure that photographs and ephemera relating to service personnel who fought in the First World War found in bookshops and at fairs which would otherwise have been lost, are preserved and made accessible. The compiler is particularly concerned with ensuring that the part played by the common man in the tumultuous events of the Great War does not go unmarked by posterity and that there is more than just a name on a war memorial to record the passing of men who fought and often died for King and Country.

The index, compiled by Simon Jervis and consisting of photographs of World War I servicemen and officers (mainly soldiers, but it does include some sailors, marines and airmen) is open for searches. Every photograph has been carefully researched and identified from the Medal Rolls and other records.

The number, rank and name is given together with the regiment or unit and details of any decorations. Details of regiment(s) and corps in which the man served are also recorded together with any subsequent renumbering. Many men served with several regiments and many who were wounded were not sent back to the trenches after convalescence, but transferred to the Labour Corps.

The index also includes other ephemera such as postcards and letters to and from the man, discharge documents, photographs of graves (often the original field grave), medal slips, Christmas cards, memorial cards and pay books.

The index has been computerised by Imperial Soldier Searches and on receipt of a cheque or postal order for £3 and a stamped, addressed, envelope (UK) or an International Money Order for £3 in sterling, self addressed envelope and two International Reply Coupons (overseas) a search will be made. If nothing is found, the enquiry will be included in the database and checked against future additions as new material is coming in all the while.

If an entry is found the enquiry will be passed to Simon Jervis who will negotiate with the enquirer direct for copies of the relevant material.

Because of the archival nature of the material, he will retain copyright of all photographs and will offer laser or photographic copies and negatives.

Remittances, payable to Imperial Soldier Searches, should be sent to Cobwebs, Long Burton, Sherborne, Dorset DT9 5PD, UK.

Readers should also be aware that there is a Photographic Archive at the Imperial War Museum (visitor's room at All Saints Annexe, Austral Street, London, 0171-416-5333, open by appointment Monday - Friday, 10.00am 5.00pm.) that has over 5 million WWI, WW2 and post-war photographs. Write to the Imperial War Museum, Lambeth Road, London SE1 6HZ .

A photograph showing the difficulty with dating photographs. This is William Edgar Leonard Lacey taken in India in 1919. He is still wearing the four stripes and crown of a Regimental Sergeant Major of the 19th century.

INDEX